CHRONICLES
of a
BO$$

Your Blueprint To Creating
a Life of
Independence
FREEDOM
& Wealth

LaToya "Toyiah Marquis" White

Bright Girl Publishing, Inc.

Cover illustration by: Julia Elliot
Design and Composition by: Julia Elliot

You can find this book and previous works by LaToya at: Amazon.com, BarnesandNoble.com, Book Stores, Libraries and the Author's official website.

www.ChroniclesofaBoss.com

Bright Girl Publishing, Inc.
ISBN-13: 978-0692523193
ISBN-10: 0692523197

LaToya "Toyiah Marquis" White is available for speaking engagements, interviews and events.
PR/Bookings Contact: Bookings@ToyiahMarquis.com

Acknowledgments

I'd like to thank God for instilling in me the ever flowing creative visions, and the guts to go get it when the world has told me I wasn't good enough. To my family, friends, and business partners for their undying love and support in my many ventures and crazy choices in life. Without you guys I don't know where I would be. My ideas, my tears, my struggles, my joys, my highs, and lows have been shared with you all at some point, and I appreciate you all so very much for allowing me to dream and for being that listening ear when I needed it most. My two heartbeats LaNiyah and Noelle for making me become a better person, showing me what life is all about and exemplifying unconditional love. To the many people that have ever called me for advice, for inspiration, and those that have hired me to get their businesses set up, you inspire me to keep going and to continue my journey of serving others. Nothing feels better than seeing the joy and excitement on your face when you become "official." Lastly, to anyone that reads this book I thank you for giving my words a chance to help shape your future. My goal is to help you break down barriers and allow you to be the best YOU possible. The time is NOW!!!

Contents

Author Introduction   6

PART I. WHO AM I AND WHY AM I HERE?   9

How to find out why you're here: What's your passion?   10
It's time to perform your self-assessment   11
Blank pages for your journaling pleasure   14

PART II. LET'S GET THIS HUSTLE STARTED!   43

Steps to starting your own business   44
Legalities: What business structure do I choose?   49
Do what you love and outsource the rest   58
The differences between copyrights, patents & trademarks   61
Business To-Do's: It's time to "Grind It Out"   68
Blank pages for your journaling pleasure   95

PART III. I'M NOT THE SAME ME I WAS WHEN I OPENED   125
        THIS BOOK

How to get out of your own way: The guide to   126
        holding yourself accountable
Fuck It! List   129
Blank pages for your journaling pleasure   131

PART IV. HOW TO GET PAID! NOW.   161

What is a profit center?   162
Diversifying: Having multiple profit centers   163
How do I manage all this stuff?   165
Blank pages for your journaling pleasure   168

PART V. I'M ON MY WAY, HOW DO I SUSTAIN?   198

Top 10 reasons why a lot of businesses fail   199
One step closer   200
Blank pages for your journaling pleasure   201

PART VI. IT'S A MENTAL THING, YOU WOULD UNDERSTAND   232

You're on your way: Affirmations   232
Creating your own personal mantra   233
Staying the course   234
Blank pages for your journaling pleasure   237

Boss'tionary, Biz Glossary   267
Resources   274

INTRODUCTION

Truth is, once you get through the mental barrage of becoming an Entrepreneur the rest is easy. At least for me it was. Starting out and working for yourself takes you through some serious emotional challenges. Some deep-rooted, soul-searching. It tugs at emotions you never knew you had. Making the decision to go at it 100% can put you at odds with a lot of people too. It truly can be a lonely road. That's why it's important to surround yourself around people that are just as crazy as you. People with the same aspirations. The doers, the go-getters, the people that understand what it's truly like to risk it all for a vision only you can see. These are the few that won't judge you. Those whom understand the struggle. I never could have imagined devoting 15 years of my life to someone else's company. But, it happened so fast. Time got away from me. It was sweet! The company made it so easy to stay, and to be comfortable. The people, the environment, the mission, the customer first spirit, upper level management and the executives were just like you and me. Reachable, likeable, learnable. (Yes, sometimes I create my own words.) To sweeten the pie even more the chairman; a self-made billionaire and real-estate mogul; I figured -- I could, AND did learn a lot from him.

So, being at this place became my adult themed safety blanket. It was February 2014, when I received my notice of layoff. It wasn't sad. I simply outgrew the position and there was nowhere else to go but out the door. July 3, 2014, was my last day. I haven't looked back since. Finally, the freedom I always longed for. I'd built several businesses, and traveled the world all while having a 9 to 5. There was so much flexibility at that place. For years I toured the world with my old R&B singing group Che, in 2006, I opened a 2500 sq. foot retail store from ground up, I traveled to and from Los Angeles, NYC, Atlanta and many states in between with musical artists that I was managing at the time, did TV/Film and a few stage plays, I helped my then 6-year old daughter, 2xs Award-winning Author, LaNiyah Bailey, become an international household name by releasing two Anti-Bullying books and leading the charge against bullying throughout the world, I even traveled to and from China several times during this stint. So, you see why I never left. But, I had to. I had a burning desire to create my own opportunities and to devote my time 100% to ventures that I built. Today, I'm doing just that. It hasn't been an easy road to say the least. But, it has been very fulfilling and rewarding to be afforded the opportunity to control my own destiny. Who would have ever thought a girl from a single-parent home growing up in the rough, city streets of Chicago would ever have the courage and the know-how to build a business? Yes, I shocked myself a few times too. This has been a long journey, I tell you. Getting here has been no easy task. Obstacles have come my way in the forms of: No, negative people, dream crushers, debt, failed relationships, death, financial hardships, disconnection notices, and business failures. But, guess what? I rolled with the punches and am here to tell you, you can achieve whatever you put your mind to. As long as you work like you're up against someone taking your place and you hustle just as much as you want to breathe. NOTHING CAN STOP YOU!

Welcome to Chronicles of a Boss: Your blueprint to creating a life of independence, freedom and wealth!

Use this book as your blueprint to finding you, your passion, and implementing it. Write your way to the freedom you deserve.

1

WHO AM I AND WHY AM I HERE?

Thank you so much for deciding to share your time with me. I'm actually happy that you picked up my book and decided to give it a try. Well, the question I pose to you today is this: "Who are you, and why are you here?" Not literally. So, let's break this down... Think about it, and let it sink in, as you repeat after me.

Here we go: "**Who am I, and why am I here?**" Not here reading these pages, but here on this Earth. Who are you? Don't tell me your name. Look deep inside yourself and tell me who you REALLY are.

List it here:
I am _____
I am _____
I am _____
I am _____
I am _____

That was easy. By now, you're seeing where I am going with this. We all have a divine purpose and knowing what that is can save us a lot of precious time and trouble. Now that you've gathered who you are tell me: Why are you here? This will help you determine your passion.

I'm here _____
I'm here _____
I'm here _____
I'm here _____
I'm here _____

Hmmm, that was GREAT!! I think you're onto something here. Congratulations! You know who you are and why you're here. Now can you tell me in a complete statement? This will be your mission:

_____
_____
_____
_____
_____
_____
_____

Your mission seems pretty dope for someone who didn't know who they "truly" were before this. **You're pretty awesome!**

Next up, I have a self-assessment that will help you get from point A to point B seamlessly. But before we get to that, I would like to try something with you. This requires a few minutes of quiet time. Here goes… Let's clear your mind from all the clutter and think about the life you'd like to live. What would that feel like? What would it look like? Where would you live? Who would be there with you?

This exercise is called, "Creative Visualization." You can spend 10 minutes per day visualizing the life you want to live. You'll be tapping into your inner-self and staking claim on what you want and getting it.

Getting to know me, my passion and my creative side!

Date: _____
Self-Assessment

1. What name will the world know me by: _____
_____
_____

2. What I believe my purpose is: _____
_____
_____

3. Who will my decisions affect: _____
_____
_____

4. What makes me smile: _____
_____
_____

5. The problem I'd like to solve in the world: _____
_____
_____

6. My passion in life is to: _____
_____
_____

7. If I died today, the mark I've left on the world would be: _____
_____
_____

8. The people I surround myself with are: _____
_____
_____

9. I would _____
_____ for FREE.

10. My biggest fear is: _____
_____
_____

11. I'm good at: _____
_____

12. I get _____ satisfaction when I help people.

13. My biggest obstacles are: _____
_____
_____

14. To me the status quo means: _____
_____
_____

15. If I could live the life I want, I would: _____
_____
_____

After this self-assessment you will be able to determine where you are at this current moment and where you aspire to be. Think about all of your answers and how you will take action to get to that place you desire.

I have a bunch of ideas, how do I decide which one goes first?

I've been here before. Believe me. When you're a creative person, you are not exempt from having thousands of ideas, some bright and some well, uhmm… not-so-bright, running through your head all day and all night trying to escape. Well, you can't do them all at once so, you'll need to decide which idea has the most potential of coming into fruition first. Write down your ideas. Or use the cool app Evernote to help you stay on top of your ideas.

Honing in on what idea goes first...

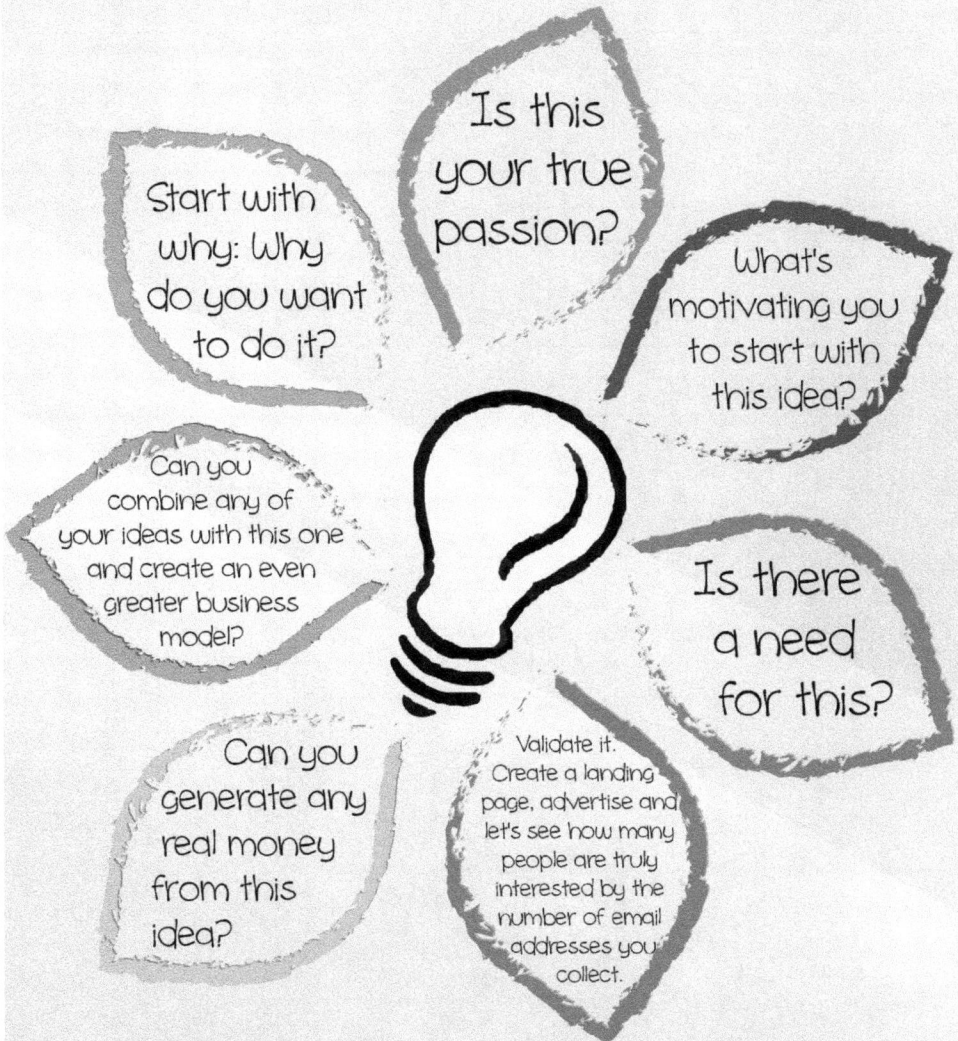

Is this your true passion?

Start with why: Why do you want to do it?

What's motivating you to start with this idea?

Can you combine any of your ideas with this one and create an even greater business model?

Is there a need for this?

Can you generate any real money from this idea?

Validate it. Create a landing page, advertise and let's see how many people are truly interested by the number of email addresses you collect.

Date: _____

Date: _____

Date: _____

Date: _____

Date: _____

Date: _____

Date: _____

Date: _____

Date: _____

Date: _____

Date: _____

Date: _____

Date: _____

Date: _____

2

LET'S GET THIS HUSTLE STARTED!

Wait…I have a question. Do you REALLY have the characteristics of a true Entrepreneur? Hmmm… Let's find out!

There are several characteristics that a true entrepreneur must possess. It takes a special type of person to be uncertain about how their bills are going to be paid a time or two, to be uncertain of the amount their next check may be… but, still be proud and just as humbled. It's funny to me because, this is the true spirit and true reality of an entrepreneur. Sounds crazy, huh? Well, can't say you were never warned. These dreamers and doers are game-changers!

As you can see being an entrepreneur requires a certain set of traits. Most people look at me and think "She's crazy" for some of the things that I do for my hustle. Some of the sacrifices that I make and for some of the not so traditional decisions that I make. But, being an entrepreneur places you in a different breed, automatically.

Some of the characteristics you must possess are:

The ability to stand the test of time…Nothing comes overnight but, a dream!

Passion: You have to be passionate about what it is that you're doing. It has to go beyond money. Realistically, we all have to eat but, at the end of the day if you're not doing something you're passionate about, you will lose! *Big time…* Passion makes getting to the finish line seeable and worthwhile.

Fire: You have to have a burning desire in your core to succeed. U have to live it, breathe it, dream it, pee it and make love to it… lol -- funny analogy but, whatev! This is my book… right?

Fearlessness: You can't be afraid of failure…You can't be afraid of the word NO. My outlook on this is: when someone tells you no, it should fuel you to create your own opportunity, not deter you from your dream.

Discipline: You must be focused on making your business work. You have to eliminate any hindrances or distractions.
You must be confident in your product and YOURSELF! Yes, I said it… *YOU!* People have to believe in you before they support your business. You should never see the glass all the way full. Be optimistic and know that

whatever it is not, it can be. You have to be willing to educate yourself more and equip yourself with more knowledge. The world changes every day so, a lot of traditional methods aren't the same anymore.

Lastly, you must **make your own rules**…And skip the status quo! Embrace change with a smile.

"There is no one size fits all to success. Don't put limitations on what you can accomplish."

The steps to starting your OWN business

So, you think you're ready to start that business? In this section I will show you the steps to go about getting that business started.

Today's date is: _____
First things first…Let's assess a few things:

What is your product or service idea? _____
_____
_____
_____
_____

Am I passionate about this? Yes or No?
If yes, why? _____
If no, CLOSE THIS CHAPTER AND START OVER!!

What will I name my business? Don't answer that… Read this first.
See below. I will give you many choices on name selection BECAUSE, there may be someone else with that same business name, doing the same thing as you. You are creative right? Well, there are others just like you and me in the world. So, don't be married to a name in the beginning stages.

Have SEVERAL choices.
Think about this:
How will this name sound when people hear it?
What does this name represent?
Does this name flow easily?
Is the name diverse?

Business names I like:

_____   _____   _____

_____   _____   _____

_____   _____   _____

Let's make sure you have free and clear usage on the name of your choice. Here's how:

Start with Google. Google the name you like and see if anyone else out there is thinking like you.

Let's do a Trademark search. Visit the USPTO website and perform a FREE TESS search to verify if anyone else has legal ownership. Here's the link: www.USPTO.gov (Trademark Search - TESS)

Check with your local Secretary of State's office to verify if someone in your state is using the name.
Who will I serve? _____
_____
_____
_____

What is my mission and vision for this business? _____
_____
_____
_____
_____

Why would anyone spend their last dollar with my business? _____
_____
_____
_____
_____

Am I doing this alone? Yes or No
If no, who will be my partner(s)? _____
_____
_____

Do they share the same vision? Yes or No
If *yes*, keep going...
If *no*, STOP RIGHT HERE!!! Think about that for a minute, let that simmer.

What about work ethic? Yes or No
If *yes*, keep going…
If *no*, STOP RIGHT HERE!!! Think about that for a minute, let that simmer.

Will they work just as hard as me or harder? Yes or No
If *yes*, keep going…
If *no*, STOP RIGHT HERE!!! Think about that for a minute, let that simmer.

What qualities do they possess? _____
_____
_____
_____

Do I/we have the money needed to start up? Yes or No
If no, where will we get this cash to start up? _____
_____
_____
_____

Where will this business be run?_____
_____
_____
_____

Will this business be part-time or full-time? _____
_____
_____
_____

CONGRATULATIONS!!
You're ready for the next step.

You're a few steps ahead of where you were before you picked up this book. I'm sure your wheels are turning now and that's great!!
But, wait… There are more IMPORTANT decisions we have to make.

Legalities: What business structure do I choose?

Welp, here comes all the legal mumbo jumbo!

Don't fret. Don't let this step intimidate you. This part is essential to how your business is legally set up. It can protect you from lawsuits, help you with tax implications, and ultimately give you the creditability you need with your consumer. It makes you "official." Believe me, deciding which business structure to choose can be a daunting task. But, somebody's got to do it, right? Let that be you.

When I consult with clients who want to start a business my biggest thing is EDUCATION. You must be educated on how your business is run. Education is key. Even though they pay me to help them get started I still try to explain to them the steps that I take to get things started for them. It's important!

Are you ready? Well, let's do this!! By the end of this discussion you will know which structure is best suited for you.

Sole Proprietorship

A sole proprietorship is the most basic type of business to establish. In a nutshell…You alone own the company and are responsible for its assets and liabilities.

You do not have to take any formal action to form a sole proprietorship. As long as you are the only owner, this status automatically comes from your business activities. In fact, you may already own one without knowing it. If you are a freelance writer, for example, you are a sole proprietor

But like all businesses, you need to obtain the necessary licenses and permits. Regulations vary by industry, state and locality. Use the Licensing & Permits tool to find a listing of federal, state and local permits, licenses and registrations you'll need to run a business.

Advantages of a Sole Proprietorship
· Easy and inexpensive to form: A sole proprietorship is the simplest and least expensive business structure to establish. Costs are minimal, with legal costs limited to obtaining the necessary license or permits.

· Complete control. Because you are the sole owner of the business, you have complete control over all decisions. You aren't required to consult with anyone else when you need to make decisions or want to make changes.

· Easy tax preparation. Your business is not taxed separately, so it's easy to fulfill the tax reporting requirements for a sole proprietorship. The tax rates are also the lowest of the business structures

Disadvantages of a Proprietorship
· Unlimited personal liability. Because there is no legal separation between you and your business, you can be held personally liable for the debts and obligations of the business. This risk extends to any liabilities incurred as a result of employee actions.

· Hard to raise money. Sole proprietors often face challenges when trying to raise money. Because you can't sell stock in the business, investors won't often invest. Banks are also hesitant to lend to a sole proprietorship because of a perceived lack of credibility when it comes to repayment if the business fails.

· Heavy burden. The flipside of complete control is the burden and pressure it can impose. You alone are ultimately responsible for the successes and failures of your business.

Limited Liability Company
An LLC is designed to provide the limited liability features of a corporation and the tax efficiencies and operational flexibility of a partnership.

A limited liability company is a hybrid type of legal structure that provides the limited liability features of a corporation and the tax efficiencies and operational flexibility of a partnership.

The "owners" of an LLC are referred to as "members." Depending on the state, the members can consist of a single individual (one owner), two or more individuals, corporations or other LLCs.

Unlike shareholders in a corporation, LLCs are not taxed as a separate business entity. Instead, all profits and losses are "passed through" the business to each member of the LLC. LLC members report profits and losses on their personal federal tax returns, just like the owners of a partnership would.

Advantages of an LLC
· Limited Liability. Members are protected from personal liability for business decisions or actions of the LLC. This means that if the LLC incurs debt or is sued, members' personal assets are usually exempt. This is similar to the liability protections afforded to shareholders of a corporation. Keep in mind that limited liability means "limited" liability - members are not necessarily shielded from wrongful acts, including those of their employees.

· Less Recordkeeping. An LLC's operational ease is one of its greatest advantages. Compared to an S-Corporation, there is less registration paperwork and there are smaller start-up costs.

· Sharing of Profits. There are fewer restrictions on profit sharing within an LLC, as members distribute profits as they see fit. Members might contribute different proportions of capital and sweat equity. Consequently, it's up to the members themselves to decide who has earned what percentage of the profits or losses.

Disadvantages of an LLC
· Limited Life. In many states, when a member leaves an LLC, the business is dissolved and the members must fulfill all remaining legal and business obligations to close the business. The remaining members can decide if they want to start a new LLC or part ways. However, you can include provisions in your operating agreement to prolong the life of the LLC if a member decides to leave the business.

· Self-Employment Taxes. Members of an LLC are considered self-employed and must pay the self-employment tax contributions towards Medicare and Social Security. The entire net income of the LLC is subject to this tax.

Cooperative
People form cooperatives to meet a collective need or to provide a service that benefits all member-owners.

A cooperative is a business or organization owned by and operated for the benefit of those using its services. Profits and earnings generated by the cooperative are distributed among the members, also known as user-owners.

Typically, an elected board of directors and officers run the cooperative while regular members have voting power to control the direction of the cooperative. Members can become part of the cooperative by purchasing shares, though the amount of shares they hold does not affect the weight of their vote.

Cooperatives are common in the healthcare, retail, agriculture, art and restaurant industries.

Corporation

A corporation is more complex and generally suggested for larger, established companies with multiple employees. Learn more about how Corporations are structured.

A corporation (sometimes referred to as a C corporation) is an independent legal entity owned by shareholders. This means that the corporation itself, not the shareholders that own it, is held legally liable for the actions and debts the business incurs.

Corporations are more complex than other business structures because they tend to have costly administrative fees and complex tax and legal requirements. Because of these issues, corporations are generally suggested for established, larger companies with multiple employees.

For businesses in that position, corporations offer the ability to sell ownership shares in the business through stock offerings. "Going public" through an initial public offering (IPO) is a major selling point in attracting investment capital and high quality employees.

Advantages of a Corporation
· Limited Liability. When it comes to taking responsibility for business debts and actions of a corporation, shareholders' personal assets are protected. Shareholders can generally only be held accountable for their investment in stock of the company.

· Ability to Generate Capital. Corporations have an advantage when it comes to raising capital for their business - the ability to raise funds through the sale of stock.

· Corporate Tax Treatment. Corporations file taxes separately from their owners. Owners of a corporation only pay taxes on corporate profits paid to them in the form of salaries, bonuses, and dividends, while any additional profits are awarded a corporate tax rate, which is usually lower than a personal income tax rate.

· Attractive to Potential Employees. Corporations are generally able to attract and hire high-quality and motivated employees because they offer competitive benefits and the potential for partial ownership through stock options.

Disadvantages of a Corporation
· Time and Money. Corporations are costly and time-consuming ventures to start and operate. Incorporating requires start-up, operating and tax costs that most other structures do not require.

· Double Taxing. In some cases, corporations are taxed twice - first, when the company makes a profit, and again when dividends are paid to shareholders.

· Additional Paperwork. Because corporations are highly regulated by federal, state, and in some cases local agencies, there are increased paperwork and recordkeeping burdens associated with this entity.

S Corporation

An S corporation is similar to a C corporation but you are taxed only on the personal level.

An S corporation (sometimes referred to as an S Corp) is a special type of corporation created through an IRS tax election. An eligible domestic corporation can avoid double taxation (once to the corporation and again to the shareholders) by electing to be treated as an S corporation.

An S corp is a corporation with the Subchapter S designation from the IRS. To be considered an S corp, you must first charter a business as a corporation in the state where it is headquartered. According to the IRS,

S corporations are "considered by law to be a unique entity, separate and apart from those who own it." This limits the financial liability for which you (the owner, or "shareholder") are responsible. Nevertheless, liability protection is limited - S corps do not necessarily shield you from all litigation such as an employee's tort actions as a result of a workplace incident.

What makes the S corp different from a traditional corporation (C corp) is that profits and losses can pass through to the personal tax return. Consequently, the business is not taxed itself. Only the shareholders are taxed. There is an important caveat, however: any shareholder who works for the company must pay him or herself "reasonable compensation." Basically, the shareholder must be paid fair market value, or the IRS might reclassify any additional corporate earnings as "wages."

Advantages of an S Corporation
· Tax Savings. One of the best features of the S Corp is the tax savings for you and your business. While members of an LLC are subject to employment tax on the entire net income of the business, only the wages of the S Corp shareholder who is an employee are subject to employment tax. The remaining income is paid to the owner as a "distribution," which is taxed at a lower rate, if at all.

· Business Expense Tax Credits. Some expenses that shareholder/employees incur can be written off as business expenses. Nevertheless, if such an employee owns 2% or more shares, then benefits like health and life insurance are deemed taxable income.

· Independent Life. An S corp designation also allows a business to have an independent life, separate from its shareholders. If a shareholder leaves the company, or sells his or her shares, the S corp can continue doing business relatively undisturbed. Maintaining the business as a distinct corporate entity defines clear lines between the shareholders and the business that improve the protection of the shareholders.

Disadvantages of an S Corporation
· Stricter Operational Processes. As a separate structure, S corps require scheduled director and shareholder meetings, minutes from those meetings, adoption and updates to by-laws, stock transfers and records maintenance.

· Shareholder Compensation Requirements. A shareholder must receive reasonable compensation. The IRS takes notice of shareholder red flags like low salary/high distribution combinations, and may reclassify your distributions as wages. You could pay a higher employment tax because of an audit with these results.

Partnership

There are several different types of partnerships, which depend on the nature of the arrangement and partner responsibility for the business.

A partnership is a single business where two or more people share ownership.

Each partner contributes to all aspects of the business, including money, property, labor or skill. In return, each partner shares in the profits and losses of the business.

Because partnerships entail more than one person in the decision-making process, it's important to discuss a wide variety of issues up front and develop a legal partnership agreement. This agreement should document how future business decisions will be made, including how the partners will divide profits, resolve disputes, change ownership (bring in new partners or buy out current partners) and how to dissolve the partnership. Although partnership agreements are not legally required, they are strongly recommended and it is considered extremely risky to operate without one.

Types of Partnerships

There are three general types of partnership arrangements:
· General Partnerships assume that profits, liability and management duties are divided equally among partners. If you opt for an unequal distribution, the percentages assigned to each partner must be documented in the partnership agreement.

· Limited Partnerships (also known as a partnership with limited liability) are more complex than general partnerships. Limited partnerships allow partners to have limited liability as well as limited input with management decisions. These limits depend on the extent of each partner's investment percentage. Limited partnerships are attractive to investors of short-term projects.

· Joint Ventures act as general partnership, but for only a limited period of time or for a single project. Partners in a joint venture can be recognized as an ongoing partnership if they continue the venture, but they must file as such.

Advantages of a Partnership

· Easy and Inexpensive. Partnerships are generally an inexpensive and easily formed business structure. The majority of time spent starting a partnership often focuses on developing the partnership agreement.

· Shared Financial Commitment. In a partnership, each partner is equally invested in the success of the business. Partnerships have the advantage of pooling resources to obtain capital. This could be beneficial in terms of securing credit, or by simply doubling your seed money.

· Complementary Skills. A good partnership should reap the benefits of being able to utilize the strengths, resources and expertise of each partner.

· Partnership Incentives for Employees. Partnerships have an employment advantage over other entities if they offer employees the opportunity to become a partner. Partnership incentives often attract highly motivated and qualified employees.

Disadvantages of a Partnership

· Joint and Individual Liability. Similar to sole proprietorships, partnerships retain full, shared liability among the owners. Partners are not only liable for their own actions, but also for the business debts and decisions made by other partners. In addition, the personal assets of all partners can be used to satisfy the partnership's debt.

· Disagreements among partners. With multiple partners, there are bound to be disagreements. Partners should consult each other on all decisions, make compromises, and resolve disputes as amicably as possible.

· Shared Profits. Because partnerships are jointly owned, each partner must share the successes and profits of their business with the other partners. An unequal contribution of time, effort, or resources can cause discord among partners.

Was that hard? I told you so. By now you should have a clearer picture on which business structure works best for your business. After this you can register your business with your state. Upon confirmation that your business has been approved you will then go to the IRS.gov website and obtain your EIN (Employer Identification Number). This is FREE. But, you must have your approval first UNLESS you choose the Sole Proprietor route. After this step you need to obtain proper licensing and/or business permits necessary to operate your business. Don't forget to talk to someone about the various types of business insurance that you may need. Don't get what you don't need.

Notes to self:

_____
_____
_____
_____
_____
_____
_____
_____
_____
_____
_____
_____
_____
_____
_____
_____
_____
_____
_____
_____
_____

"Do what you love and outsource the rest!"

What exactly am I saying here?

What I'm saying is that in business you can't be all things. You can't be the cashier, the accountant, the secretary, the social media strategist, the janitor, the graphic designer, AND the customer service rep.

Technically, you can. But why drain yourself and diminish your productivity? Why place added pressure and stress on yourself? Stop here!

It's ok to understand the processes behind each step and to be educated. But, in today's world there are so many resources available to us that it just makes more sense to hire someone else to handle the tasks.

Why do the boring shit that makes you cringe upon thinking about it? There's hope!!

Efficiency is especially critical to entrepreneurs, we must learn self-discipline to ensure the freedom of creating our own schedules. We don't have a boss hovering over us and telling us when something has to be done. In knowing this, we have to ensure our time is being spent doing things of value.
Simply put:

"If you don't hustle, you don't eat."

Sometimes we find that there are hundreds of jumbled tasks that come with running our own business. These tasks tend to be tedious and unexciting, and they eat away your precious time. Time that you could be doing much more valuable things with. But these things must be done. So, you can't just forget about them. This is where outsourcing comes in.

Consider this:
While running a business, we typically have the few things we love to do and the things we are good at. This may be writing content, making sales calls, working with customers, designing new products, working on the website, etc. To you these are considered the big tasks that appear to be the

important stuff in your business. But then we have all the stupid little tasks that we probably do not enjoy doing. This may be any of the listed above items, or it could be simpler tasks like checking and returning emails, updating files, recording data, book keeping, etc. Basically, we have a few things that we would love to do in our business all the time, and we have the rest of it which we would prefer not to deal with, but must, because our business couldn't survive without it.

Below I will share with you the platforms in which there is HELP for you.

You can thank me by sending an email to me at: Toyiah@ToyiahMarquis.com I take tips...hahaha

Fiverr
Web Address: www.Fiverr.com
Services on Fiverr start at just $5.
You can browse through the millions of Gigs available and order exactly what you need: from logos, graphic design, article writing, ad copy, virtual assistance, and even weirder tasks can be purchased here. Make sure you pay attention to seller ratings. Much like eBay this feedback will allow you to determine if this seller would be of value to you or a headache. And who needs a headache? Not you. Protect your time. Oh yeah, you must have a PayPal account setup to pay for your gigs.

Upwork
Web Address: www.Upwork.com
What kind of work can I get done using Upwork?
Anything that can be done on a computer – from web and mobile programming to graphic design – can be done on Upwork. Freelance experts can tackle a range of projects:
> · Big or small
> · Short or ongoing
> · Individual or team-based

Whether you need a writer to knock out a 500-word blog post or a full-fledged software development team to support your business, Upworks tools and the expert freelancers in their marketplace can accommodate.

How do I hire the right freelancer? Start by writing a clear and concise job post. Each freelancer submits a cover letter and link to their Upwork profile covering:

- Skills, experience and portfolios
- Client feedback ← Pay attention to this!! It will stop you from wasting time. We don't waste our time around here.
- Language and communication skills ← Can this person understand your language? Can they write to where it makes sense to your customer? This is very important.

It's easy. You'll get applications from independent professionals and receive our personalized recommendations within minutes. From there, just interview your strongest candidates and hire your favorite.

How do payments work?
Pay your freelancer per hour or per project, whichever you choose.
Choose from the following billing methods:
- Credit card
- PayPal
- Bank account

When Upwork sends your payments to the freelancer, they deduct a 10% fee from the rate they charge you. For example, if you pay your freelancer $20, Freelancer earns $18 and Upwork will receive $2.

99 Designs

Web Address: www.99designs.com
On 99 Designs you can launch a contest which lets a community of more than 1,080,000 designers view your contest. From Berlin to Bombay, professional creatives will read your brief and begin to brainstorm ideas just for you. Anything from a logo, product packaging, book cover design, website, app creation and much more!!
99 Designs offers a bronze, silver, gold and platinum package for you to choose from. Quite naturally it comes with a price. But, it's your budget you decide which option best suits your needs.
Pick the winner
After 7 days, you can pick the winner and sign a copyright agreement.
99 Designs will transfer the prize money to the designer. Then you can download your new design and use it however you like.
It's that simple.

I hope I've given you the resources that will help your business succeed.
I personally use all three platforms and I'm smiling!!

The difference between: Copyrights, Patents, and Trademarks: Oh My...

So, someone told you, you could mail yourself an envelope and it would be alright? Yes?

NOT! Just not possible. This is often referred to as the "Poor Man's" copyright. This method does not offer protection on your intellectual property. One must present his or her federal copyright registration to sue for infringement.

So, in short save yourself an envelope, a stamp and your valuable time and do it the right way.

Did you think you could copyright your business name? Nope, that's NOT copyrightable!

Let's get down to the BizzzNess: Here goes.

Some people confuse patents, copyrights, and trademarks. Although there may be some similarities among these kinds of intellectual property protection, they are different and serve different purposes.
So, I will break down the differences for each type of intellectual property protection so you'll know which route you need to go in to protect your asset.

Copyrights

What is copyright?
Copyright is a form of protection grounded in the U.S. Constitution and granted by law for original works of authorship fixed in a tangible medium of expression. Copyright covers both published and unpublished works.

What does copyright protect?
Copyright, a form of intellectual property law, protects original works of authorship including literary, dramatic, musical, and artistic works, such as poetry, books, movies, songs, computer software, and architecture. Copyright does not protect facts, titles, names, ideas, systems, or methods of operation, although it may protect the way these things are expressed.

How is a copyright different from a patent or a trademark?
Copyright protects original works of authorship, while a patent protects inventions or discoveries. Ideas and discoveries are not protected by the copyright law, although the way in which they are expressed may be. A trademark protects words, phrases, symbols, or designs identifying the source of the goods or services of one party and distinguishing them from those of others.

When is my work protected?
Your work is under copyright protection the moment it is created and fixed in a tangible form that it is perceptible either directly or with the aid of a machine or device.

Where do I go to register for a copyright?
You can visit the Library of Congress website and register your works here: http://copyright.gov/eco/

Patents

What is a Patent?
A patent for an invention is the grant of a property right to the inventor, issued by the United States Patent and Trademark Office. Generally, the term of a new patent is 20 years from the date on which the application for the patent was filed in the United States or, in special cases, from the date an earlier related application was filed, subject to the payment of maintenance fees. U.S. patent grants are effective only within the United States, U.S. territories, and U.S. possessions. Under certain circumstances, patent term extensions or adjustments may be available.

The right conferred by the patent grant is, in the language of the statute and of the grant itself, "the right to exclude others from making, using, offering for sale, or selling" the invention in the United States or "importing" the invention into the United States. What is granted is not the right to make, use, offer for sale, sell or import, but the right to exclude others from making, using, offering for sale, selling or importing the invention. Once a patent is issued, the patentee must enforce the patent without aid of the USPTO.

There are three types of patents:

1) Utility patents may be granted to anyone who invents or discovers any new and useful process, machine, article of manufacture, or composition of matter, or any new and useful improvement thereof;
2) Design patents may be granted to anyone who invents a new, original, and ornamental design for an article of manufacture; and
3) Plant patents may be granted to anyone who invents or discovers and asexually reproduces any distinct and new variety of plant.

What can be Patented?
Under U.S. patent law, any person who "invents or discovers any new and useful process, machine, manufacture, or composition of matter, or any new and useful improvement thereof, may obtain a patent." In general, this means you must satisfy the following four requirements to qualify for a patent:
· The subject matter must be patentable.
· The invention must be novel.
· The invention must have some utility or usefulness.
· The invention must not be obvious.

Patentable subject matter
A patent cannot protect an idea. Instead, the idea must be embodied in one or more of the following:
· A process or method (such as a new way to manufacture concrete)
· A machine (something with moving parts or circuitry)
· A manufactured article (such as a tool or another object that accomplishes a result with few or no moving parts, such as a pencil)
· A new composition (such as a new pharmaceutical)
· An asexually reproduced and new variety of plant.

Even if the invention falls into one of the four above categories, there are certain subject matters that cannot be patented. These include mathematical formulas, naturally-occurring substances, laws of nature and processes done entirely with the human body (such as a technique for shooting a free throw in basketball).

Where do I go to register for a Patent?
You can visit the USPTO office website here: http://www.uspto.gov/patents-getting-started/general-information-concerning-patents#heading-12

Trademarks & Service Marks

What Is a Trademark or Service Mark and How Do They Differ From Patents and Copyrights?
A trademark is a brand name. A trademark or service mark includes any word, name, symbol, device, or any combination, used or intended to be used to identify and distinguish the goods/services of one seller or provider from those of others, and to indicate the source of the goods/services.

Should I Register My Trademark?
Although federal registration of a mark is not mandatory, it has several advantages, including notice to the public of the registrant's claim of ownership of the mark, legal presumption of ownership nationwide, and exclusive right to use the mark on or in connection with the goods/services listed in the registration.

But wait…Before you file a Trademark it is IMPORTANT that you search: www.USPTO.gov TESS database before filing your application, to determine whether anyone already claims trademark rights in a particular mark through a federal registration. Failure to conduct a proper search may result in your not making a proper assessment as to whether an application should even be filed and your fees are NOT refundable.

Perform your Trademark search
Here's the link and good luck! http://tmsearch.uspto.gov/
I hope that I've shed some light on the various types of IP protection there is and that you've been able to identify which one is right for you.

Copyrights, Patents & Trademarks

What did I learn?

My creative works that can be copyrighted are:

1. _____
2. _____
3. _____
4. _____
5. _____
6. _____
7. _____
8. _____
9. _____
10. _____

My invention(s) that I would like to see patented are:

1. _____
2. _____
3. _____
4. _____
5. _____
6. _____
7. _____
8. _____
9. _____
10. _____

My product(s) and/or service(s) that can be trademarked are:

1. _____
2. _____
3. _____
4. _____
5. _____
6. _____
7. _____
8. _____
9. _____
10. _____

Great!!
Now you've got the concept. You're on your way!

NEXT UP:
Business To-do's

Procrastination kills dreams and time.

"Tackle This...Tackle That"

Having a to-do list is important because, we all have those days where we have so much to do and so little time to accomplish it. This causes us to lose focus and become unmotivated. It's easy to get lost in the shuffle. So, having a to-do list helps you become accountable for what it is that you have to do.

It also helps you stay organized. Why waste time on trivial activities when there are important matters that need your attention? Having a to-do list allows you to sort out your tasks and prioritize based on their importance.

As you complete your day to day tasks you start to feel motivated and happy that you've accomplished something. For me having a to-do list is a natural STRESS RELIEVER!!

We all need to de-stress sometimes and having a to-do list is the way to go.

Let's Grind It All Out...

25 pages to help you track your productivity.

Grind Time

Who do I need to call?   Date:

Who do I need to email?   Date:

What errands do I need to run?   Date:

What projects do I have?   Date:

Small miscellaneous tasks   Date:

Grind Time

Who do I need to call?   Date:

Who do I need to email?   Date:

What errands do I need to run?   Date:

What projects do I have?   Date:

Small miscellaneous tasks   Date:

Grind Time

Who do I need to call?   Date:

Who do I need to email?   Date:

What errands do I need to run?   Date:

What projects do I have?   Date:

Small miscellaneous tasks   Date:

Grind Time

Who do I need to call?   Date:

Who do I need to email?   Date:

What errands do I need to run?   Date:

What projects do I have?   Date:

Small miscellaneous tasks   Date:

Grind Time

Who do I need to call?   Date:

Who do I need to email?   Date:

What errands do I need to run?   Date:

What projects do I have?   Date:

Small miscellaneous tasks   Date:

Grind Time

Who do I need to call?   Date:

Who do I need to email?   Date:

What errands do I need to run?   Date:

ERRANDS

What projects do I have?   Date:

Projects

Small miscellaneous tasks   Date:

misc

Grind Time

Who do I need to call?   Date:

Who do I need to email?   Date:

What errands do I need to run?   Date:

ERRANDS

What projects do I have?   Date:

Projects

Small miscellaneous tasks   Date:

MISC

Grind Time

Who do I need to call?   Date:

Who do I need to email?   Date:

What errands do I need to run?   Date:

What projects do I have?   Date:

Small miscellaneous tasks   Date:

Grind Time

Who do I need to call?   Date:

Who do I need to email?   Date:

What errands do I need to run?   Date:

What projects do I have?   Date:

Small miscellaneous tasks   Date:

Grind Time

Who do I need to call?   Date:

Who do I need to email?   Date:

What errands do I need to run?   Date:

ERRANDS

What projects do I have?   Date:

Projects

Small miscellaneous tasks   Date:

misc

Grind Time

Who do I need to call?   Date:

Who do I need to email?   Date:

What errands do I need to run?   Date:

What projects do I have?   Date:

Small miscellaneous tasks   Date:

Grind Time

Who do I need to call?   Date:

Who do I need to email?   Date:

What errands do I need to run?   Date:

What projects do I have?   Date:

Small miscellaneous tasks   Date:

Grind Time

Who do I need to call?   Date:

Who do I need to email?   Date:

What errands do I need to run?   Date:

ERRANDS

What projects do I have?   Date:

Projects

Small miscellaneous tasks   Date:

mi/c

Grind Time

Who do I need to call?   Date:

Who do I need to email?   Date:

What errands do I need to run?   Date:

-ERRANDS-

What projects do I have?   Date:

Projects

Small miscellaneous tasks   Date:

misc

Grind Time

Who do I need to call?   Date:

Who do I need to email?   Date:

What errands do I need to run?   Date:

ERRANDS

What projects do I have?   Date:

Projects

Small miscellaneous tasks   Date:

misc

Grind Time

Who do I need to call?   Date:

Who do I need to email?   Date:

What errands do I need to run?   Date:

What projects do I have?   Date:

Small miscellaneous tasks   Date:

Grind Time

Who do I need to call?   Date:

Who do I need to email?   Date:

What errands do I need to run?   Date:

What projects do I have?   Date:

Small miscellaneous tasks   Date:

Grind Time

Who do I need to call? Date:

Who do I need to email? Date:

What errands do I need to run? Date:

What projects do I have? Date:

Small miscellaneous tasks Date:

Grind Time

Who do I need to call?   Date:

Who do I need to email?   Date:

What errands do I need to run?   Date:

What projects do I have?   Date:

Small miscellaneous tasks   Date:

Grind Time

Who do I need to call?   Date:

Who do I need to email?   Date:

What errands do I need to run?   Date:

What projects do I have?   Date:

Small miscellaneous tasks   Date:

Grind Time

Who do I need to call?   Date:

Who do I need to email?   Date:

What errands do I need to run?   Date:

What projects do I have?   Date:

Small miscellaneous tasks   Date:

Grind Time

Who do I need to call?   Date:

Who do I need to email?   Date:

What errands do I need to run?   Date:

What projects do I have?   Date:

Small miscellaneous tasks   Date:

Grind Time

Who do I need to call?   Date:

Who do I need to email?   Date:

What errands do I need to run?   Date:

ERRANDS

What projects do I have?   Date:

Projects

Small miscellaneous tasks   Date:

MISC

Grind Time

Who do I need to call?   Date:

Who do I need to email?   Date:

What errands do I need to run?   Date:

What projects do I have?   Date:

Small miscellaneous tasks   Date:

‡92‡

Grind Time

Who do I need to call?   Date:

Who do I need to email?   Date:

What errands do I need to run?   Date:

-ERRANDS-

What projects do I have?   Date:

Projects

Small miscellaneous tasks   Date:

misc

H.U.S.T.L.E

HAVING
UNWAVERING
STRENGTH
to THRIVE
LEAD and
EMPOWER

Date: _____

Date: _____

Date: _____

Date: _____

Date: _____

Date: _____

Date: _____

Date: _____

Date: _____

Date: _____

Date: _____

3

I'M NOT THE SAME ME THAT I WAS WHEN I OPENED THIS BOOK

How to get out of your own way: The guide to holding yourself accountable!

A lot of times we say we want to be successful, we want to live a certain lifestyle, and we would do anything to go out and get it. Right? But, deep down inside we're not even close to living up to it. Our mindset won't let us. Oftentimes, we are so afraid of success that we tell ourselves "It could never happen to me." Subconsciously, we really start to believe it. That mindset then hinders us. It prohibits us from living a life of fullness, a life of prosperity and a life that only we can master.

We are creatures of habit. So, living a certain lifestyle and believing certain things for a long period of time conditions our mind to think that we aren't supposed to have the better things in life, we aren't supposed to connect with people on different levels than ourselves, we're supposed to sit in a cubicle until we turn 65 or 67, (one of em), you begin to put crazy limitations on yourself, which then places you in a box. A box of fear, a box of standing still, and a box of failing yourself. A bunch of should haves, could haves and would haves. Why let yourself down like that? We are all here for a bigger purpose. I'm not sure what your divine purpose is but, if you're reading this book I'm sure it's in the direction of serving people and living out a life full of happiness.

That's the life we all want right? Then why stand there? GET OUT OF YOUR OWN WAY!!!

Let go of the fear, the doubt, and the limitations!

Let's do this together. I'm not here to point fingers at you. I'm truly here to help you get a jumpstart on living a life of independence, freedom, and wealth. Just a girl from the Westside of Chicago living out her mission of helping others. Yes, I made it this far and now I'm FINALLY able to put my thoughts into action and to help you, and others like you who want to make a difference in the world.

Fact is: I'm helping myself as well. We're in this TOGETHER!

Truth is we all have come up with excuses as to why productivity is down. And we've all told ourselves we'd get to it and never did. Holding ourselves accountable can really help us progress. The best way to hold yourself accountable is to have a repeatable system that you can follow on a day-to-day basis that allows you to measure your results, to know whether you are cultivating, going nowhere or reverting.

Here's a few ways you can move forward and start achieving the success you desire.

Winning ways to hold yourself accountable and become the WINNER you are:

▷ Use your to-do list on a daily basis to write down your tasks. Doing this makes you stay focused on what you need to do and how you need to spend your time.

▷ Write down your ideas. When we have ideas in our head writing them down can help with fueling the fire of actually implementing that idea. Keep a notepad or this journal by your bed to take notes.

▷ Hand some things over. Delegate some of your smaller tasks. You can outsource or even find a few interns to help out. This frees up your valuable time and allows you to focus on the bigger tasks at hand.

▷ Set deadlines. We can't be walking around like a zombie with no deadlines. When you set deadlines you are making yourself aware that imperative things need to be done. Oftentimes, when we miss scheduled deadlines we get disappointed with ourselves. So, the next go round we stay on course. It's a mind thing. But, I like it!

▷ Stop dreaming and start doing. Put your plans into action. Start that business, write that book, create that invention, or write that hit song. It's all about implementation. If you don't you'll have that "should've, would've" disease later on in life. Take action!!

▷ You can't get there by yourself. Let's learn to put our pride to the side and ask for help. Asking for help doesn't make you weak. It actually makes you stronger because, you realized that you can't do it all by yourself.

▷ Get yourself a mentor. A mentor can be a great accountability partner.

A mentor is someone who's already achieved what you've set out to achieve for yourself. A great mentor has already experienced important lessons that he or she can share with you to help you grow personally and professionally. Your mentor becomes your tour guide on your journey to success.

▷ Create a clear vision for your life. Once we paint that picture of where we truly want our life to be, we work hard to get there.

▷ Think about who may be affected by your finances and your life decisions. It could be your children, your spouse, or your family members. Think about if you gave up how it would affect them. There you have it! Giving up is not an option.

I hope these tips gave you a better insight on why it is important to hold yourself accountable. Once you start executing these steps you'll notice a change. Your reasons for whatever it is you do become clearer. You begin to value your time and others' time. Those little nuisances become non-factors.

Where's my bucket list?

Uh, Oh! …Not today

It's the opposite!

Fuck It! List

I want you to think about all the things that discourage you from living the life you want to live. All the negative thoughts, things, and maybe even people. Ok?

Now let's add those to your fuck it, list.   Date: _____

_____
_____
_____
_____
_____
_____
_____
_____
_____
_____
_____
_____
_____
_____
_____
_____
_____
_____
_____
_____

Didn't that feel good? Keep adding. Pretty soon it'll be full, and there will be nothing standing in your way but, space and opportunity!!!!

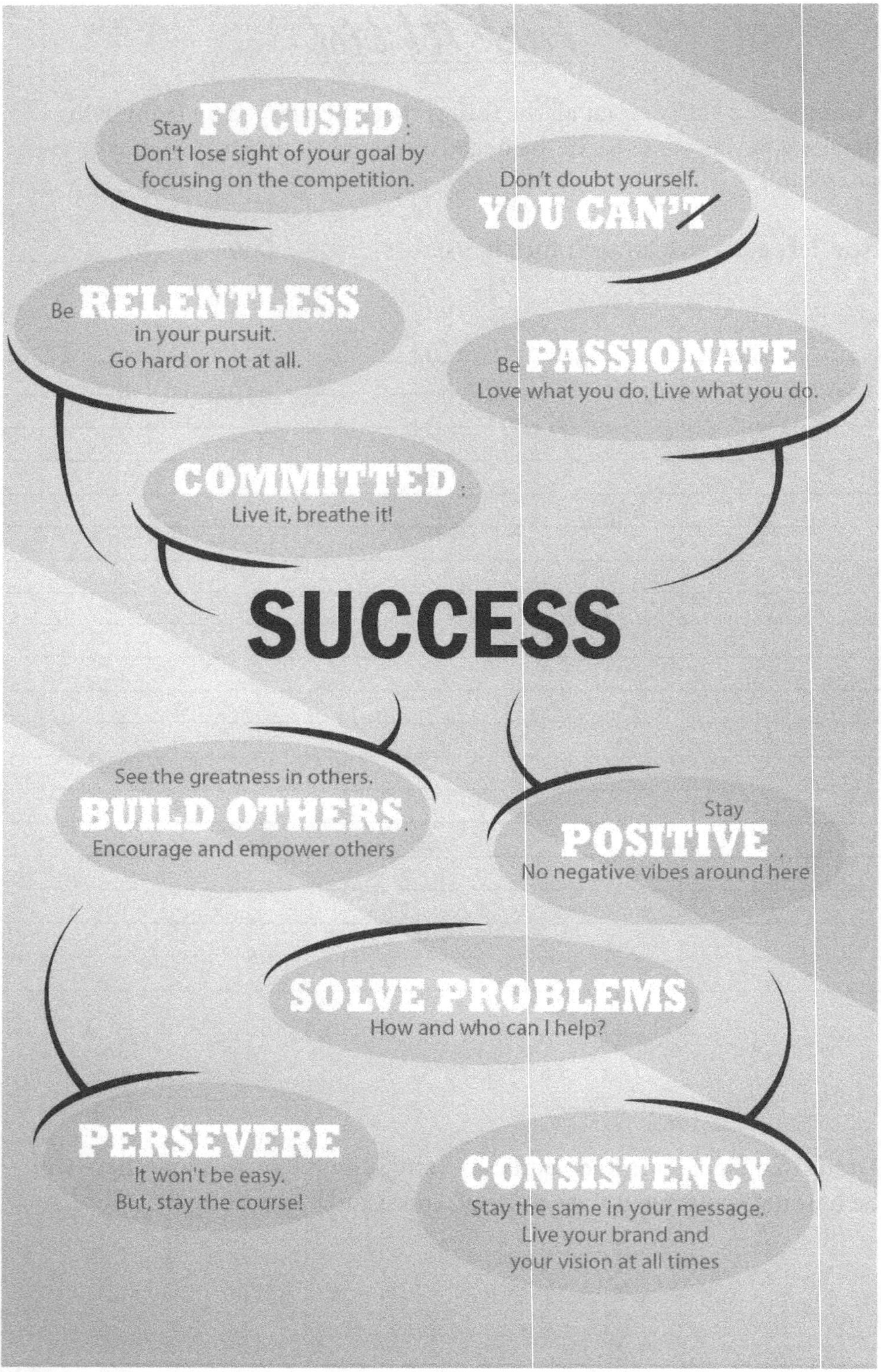
Stay FOCUSED:
Don't lose sight of your goal by focusing on the competition.
Don't doubt yourself.
YOU CAN'T
Be RELENTLESS
in your pursuit.
Go hard or not at all.
Be PASSIONATE
Love what you do. Live what you do.
COMMITTED:
Live it, breathe it!
SUCCESS
See the greatness in others.
BUILD OTHERS.
Encourage and empower others
Stay
POSITIVE.
No negative vibes around here
SOLVE PROBLEMS.
How and who can I help?
PERSEVERE
It won't be easy.
But, stay the course!
CONSISTENCY
Stay the same in your message.
Live your brand and
your vision at all times

Date: _____

Date: _____

Date: _____

Date: _____

Date: _____

Date: _____

Date: _____

Date: _____

Date: _____

Date: _____

Date: _____

4

HOW TO GET PAID!
NOW!

What is a Profit Center?

When you're just starting out as an entrepreneur it can be a little challenging, financially. Especially when you don't know what your next paycheck is going to amount to. So, it is very important that you have multiple streams of income coming in. I'd like to call you a "Chef" with multiple recipes. This helps you during those slow moments when income isn't flowing the same. It won't be this way EVERY month, but trust me: some months you'll be eating ramen noodles and cheese. That's if you like cheese. Hahaha... You get it though!

Let's take Dunkin Donuts for instance. They are known for selling donuts and coffee. Well, during the summer months the selling of hot coffee decreases because, people want to stay cool in the summer. Dunkin Donuts noticed the trend. They then added iced coffee and frozen drinks to their menu. This added an additional leg of revenue. Get it? So, now do you see where I'm going with this? It's called diversifying your income. I learned a lot about this in my favorite book called "Making a Living without a Job" by Barbara Winter. In the book Barbara talks a lot about how to survive being "joyfully, jobless." This book is a staple on my book shelf. It opened my eyes to the thought of tackling multiple streams of income.

I used to be embarrassed to tell people that I did so many things. Because, I felt like they'd judge me, and coin me as a "jack of all trades, master of none" but, that would be furthest from the truth. What I was doing was ensuring me and my children were able to eat every month. And at the same time I was doing everything effectively and efficiently. Because, I have a team it's much easier. We talked about taking on a team earlier in the book. This is an important element to diversifying and growing a business, hands down.

Adding a new leg to your business or offering a new product to your collection are great ways to start out. I am not saying add a million things to your plate at once.

What I am recommending is that you add one thing at a time. Maximize that one thing. Become an expert in it. Pull together a team for this task to make sure there are no flaws in the system and then you can add an additional ingredient to your recipe. To start on the next leg. Understand? You can't juggle 10 balls by yourself. You CAN juggle one at a time.

Diversifying: Having Multiple Profit Centers

You can create your profit centers to revolve around your current business or you can create completely unrelated streams. The bottom line is making sure it works for you AND that you are passionate about doing them.

Here's an example of how we pulled profit centers from our cosmetics line "So She Cosmetics" (www.SoSheCosmetics.com) While we started off as a cosmetics company in 2008, that offered a full-line of color cosmetics we felt like we had to do more for when times got slow on us. Well, we then decided to teach basic make-up application to women who wanted to learn the basics of applying makeup. After that we noticed that more and more of our customers were asking if we applied makeup as well. So, we studied long and hard, practiced, messed up a few faces, researched the fundamentals of becoming a Makeup Artist, and perfected many... WALA! We rolled out our Makeup Artistry. We began freelancing throughout the Midwest. Doing Fashion Shows, Magazines, TV/Film shoots and weddings. People were calling and we were delivering every time. And at all times we wore our own branded aprons and only used our products.

This gave every person we applied makeup to the opportunity to try out our makeup, firsthand. If they liked it a lot, we were able to convert them into loyal customers. If not, we still had the pleasure of serving them.

We then added a home party side to it, because, we know that home parties are the "in thing" these days. Girls' night outs, bridal showers, birthday parties, get away from the kids and spouse parties – "Pretty Parties" were born!! Women LOVED the concept. We added so many bells and whistles to it that you couldn't pass it up. As our demand grew women started asking for more and more. We listened to our customers and we heard them loud and clear! Most of them had issues with finding the right foundation to match their skin. WALA again!! We added a FREE foundation matching service. Where women could come in to our office and we'd match them up with the correct color for their skin. Another leg we pulled out of the brand has been independent sales reps by way of other makeup artists and individuals who just love makeup and believe they can stand on a brand that really does what it says. And finally we've introduced "collections." Reaching out to influencers and offering them their own collections under our brand name has shown us that the sky is truly the limit. Now as you can see we have pulled several profit centers from our one business. This is called "clustered profit centers."

Did I make you tired? Ha! As you can now imagine you can do the SAME thing. It's easy. Just allow your creativity to do its part. You will definitely figure it out.

Not every concept works for everyone and this I totally understand. If you can't seem to pull anything from your current business to create clusters you can go another route to diversify.

Ask yourself this:

What additional legs can I pull from my current business? _____
_____
_____
_____

Your wheels must be turning now. I will give you more room.

_____
_____
_____
_____
_____
_____

Can I consult people on how to do what I do? If yes, what?

_____
_____
_____
_____
_____
_____

Can I teach others ANYTHING that relates to what I do? If yes, what kind of classes can I offer and to whom?

_____

_____

_____

_____

_____

_____

There's nothing that I can pull from my current business. But, I think I can create profit centers by doing: _____

_____

_____

_____

_____

Awesome! I think you're well on your way. Pretty soon, you'll be emailing me and telling me how you've maximized your abilities to create multiple streams of income. I'd love to hear it.

Now, the BIG question must be:
Toyiah, how do I manage all this stuff?

The simple way for me to break this down would be: Do everything with passion, and take it one step at a time. You'll soon create your own system and things will begin to flow perfectly. What works for you may not work for someone else. So, staying focused is the biggest component to making this all work. It's also about trial and error. Seeing what works best for you. Once you've conquered that, the rest will become second nature. And please don't be afraid to do away with things that aren't working. If you find yourself creating profit centers that don't work, don't spend too much time on it and never be afraid to "ditch it" and try something else. You can 100% of the time avoid this step by validating your market. How many people can you serve? Is there a demand for this?

-Well, that's it! I hope I've left you with enough to think about. -

Set Goals.
Make Plans.
Hustle Hard.
Make It Happen.
REPEAT!!!

ENTREPRENEURS BE LIKE...

Date: _____

Date: _____

Date: _____

Date: _____

Date: _____

Date: _____

Date: _____

Date: _____

Date: _____

Date: _____

Date: _____

5

I'M ON MY WAY,
HOW DO I SUSTAIN?

So, by now the fire is burning and you are ready to go all the way!

I commend you. Being an entrepreneur takes guts and a LOT of valor. We're the doers, the go-getters, the crazy folks that believe we have what it takes to change the world.

Guess what? We do!!

Of all my years in business I've learned some key things that have helped me.
I can now share these things with you in hopes that it keeps you from making the same mistakes myself and others have. By all means I'm not saying that making a mistake is bad. And I am not professing that in business there is a 'one size fits all.' But, there are some things I wish I would have been told before hitting my head and falling on my ass real hard a few times. (Pun intended)

Here is my list of **top 10-reasons why most businesses fail:**

1. Failure to validate the market for your product or service.
2. Trying to be all things in the business. Failing to build a team or to delegate tasks.
3. Scaling too fast.
4. Undervaluing your products and/or services.
5. Worrying about the other guy. Your competition.
6. Being afraid to let go of something that isn't working.
7. Not having enough capital from the start and/or spending revenue without covering expenses FIRST.
8. A lack of valuable resources.
9. Little to no marketing.
10. Poor customer service. Not considering the consumers wants and needs.

You're one step closer than you were yesterday.

Keep Going!

Date: _____

Date: _____

Date: _____

Date: _____

Date: _____

Date: _____

Date: _____

Date: _____

Date: _____

Date: _____

Date: _____

Date: _____

Date: _____

Date: _____

6

IT'S A MENTAL THING,
YOU WOULD UNDERSTAND

It's true that when we change our thinking we can change our lives, for the positive. Once we let go of negative thinking habits we begin the journey to transforming our lives into something great. I can't lie when you grow up without affection, feeling loved, being told YOU CAN accomplish anything in life that you desire, and being told "I love you," it is a hard and painful process to change. It's hard to change because, when you're so used to something… Change can be intimidating. Painful because, we're so afraid of being vulnerable and allowing others to see us in that light. Society makes us think that it is weak to let go, and to be open to change. Actually, it is courageous to be able to accept change and to have an open mind about it. One thing I have learned though is you have to really believe what you are saying and thinking. If you don't you're just chanting words with no passion behind them.

Affirmations fortify us by helping us to believe in the potential of an action we desire to visualize. When we verbally confirm our dreams and ambitions, we are instantly empowered with a deep sense of reassurance that our aspiring words will become reality. I am positive that using affirmations on a daily basis not only help you in your personal life but, it helps you thrive in business as well.

Here are a few affirmations I've found to be quite helpful.

1. I am the owner of me. I control my own thoughts and what gets instilled in me.
2. **I am worth it!**
3. I have a beautiful spirit.
4. Whatever I put my mind to, I can achieve.
5. I am talented beyond belief and I will share it with the world.
6. I love me just the way I am.
7. I am strong and courageous.
8. I have the power to control and change my circumstances.
9. I flow with compassion to erase hate, anger, and guilt.
10. I am a pioneer of life-changing ideas.
11. **I choose happiness. My happiness is relative to my own successes and accomplishments.**
12. I will grow and sustain my business.
13. I am not afraid of being great!
14. I am blessed with incredible family, friends, and business partners.
15. I own my confidence. I am worth it!

16. Hard times are not forever. Difficult times will remain for only a SHORT period of time.
17. **I envision my future to be bright and awesome.**
18. I am rich in spirit, character, and finances.
19. I am wealthy.
20. I radiate beauty, style and charm.
21. My smile speaks volumes. I do it often.
22. **My fears are behind me.**
23. I am at peace with my past.
24. My destiny is controlled by me.
25. I will create my own opportunities. I will remove all limitations and obstacles that stand before me.

That sounded good didn't it? Hearing yourself affirm those positive words about yourself can make a world of difference in how you feel at the moment. It can also carry over into the next day. That's why daily affirming of these positive thoughts are great. Positivity feels awesome! You are awesome and you deserve to live the life you imagine. In my journey for greatness I've followed plenty of millionaires and billionaires and that one "common denominator" was they all believe in the power of positive thinking. They all studied the art of positive thinking and creating their own success mantras. A mantra can be one word or many words. It will become your own tagline. Your mantra is an affirmation you can use to help you refocus and become a better version of yourself.

Now it's your turn. Let's create your own personal mantra.

Date: _____

_____
_____
_____
_____
_____
_____
_____
_____
_____
_____
_____

"Staying the course"

We're all human and we know that life happens. Life has a way of throwing us curve balls. But, it's up to us on how we handle it. In order to stay on a healthy path of motivation and staying focused we have to instill positivity in our minds and assure ourselves that if anything comes our way that is not satisfying to our life we have to let it go. This is the one true way that allows us to stay the course.

Staying the course requires motivation. When you're striving for greatness your days and nights can become challenging. You'll suffer from loneliness, and on some days you'll even want to give up. And I can promise you that nothing great comes easy. For me staying motivated comes in the form of reading and listening to people who inspire me. In the world of YouTube you can find 1,000's of videos that will help you stay motivated. I have a list of people that I'm inspired by. Every day I dedicate at least 45 minutes to reading articles, researching and/or watching motivational videos. I think one great way to do it is to create yourself a list of inspirations. This definitely will help you. You can watch their videos, read their articles, and buy their books so, when you need a lift, it's there at your fingertips. If you can't think of anyone in particular try reading blogs and watching videos from people in the same field you want to go in. There are millions of resources at your disposal all you have to do is GO GET IT!!!

I will help you out a little. I'm going to share my list and maybe you'll pull from mine or create your own.

Come on... Let's get to it!

Here's my list:

Alan Watts	Barbara Corcoran
Daymond John	Les Brown
Mark Cuban	Oprah Winfrey
Sam Zell	Sean Ogle
Simon Sinek	Tierra Destiny Reid
Tim Nybo & Nick Ramil	Tory Johnson
Tyler Perry	Tyrese Gibson
Will Smith	

Your turn.

Today's Date is: _____

The people that inspire me are:

1. _____
2. _____
3. _____
4. _____
5. _____
6. _____
7. _____
8. _____
9. _____
10. _____
11. _____
12. _____
13. _____
14. _____
15. _____
16. _____
17. _____
18. _____
19. _____
20. _____

Stay the Curse

It'll all be worth it!

Date: _____

Date: _____

Date: _____

Date: _____

Date: _____

Date: _____

Date: _____

Date: _____

Date: _____

Date: _____

Date: _____

Date: _____

Date: _____

Date: _____

Date: _____

Date: _____

Boss'tionary

Here you'll find 50 words that are often used in business. While these aren't all, I'm sharing with you the terms I've known to be essential.

Accounting - It is a systematic process of identifying, recording, measuring, classifying, verifying, summarizing, interpreting and communicating financial information. It reveals profit or loss for a given period, and the value and nature of a firm's assets, liabilities and owners' equity.

Advertisement - Paid, non-personal, public communication about causes, goods and services, ideas, organizations, people, and places, through means such as direct mail, telephone, print, radio, television, and internet. An integral part of marketing, advertisements are public notices designed to inform and motivate. Their objective is to change the thinking pattern (or buying behavior) of the recipient, so that he or she is persuaded to take the action desired by the advertiser. When aired on radio or television, an advertisement is called a commercial.

Annual Report - Presentation of a firm's audited accounts for the preceding year, as required in corporate legislation. In addition to the auditor's report, an annual report commonly includes (1) management's review of the operations of the firm and its future prospects, (2) balance sheet, (3) income statement (profit and loss account), (4) cash flow statement, and other supporting documents.

Asset - Something valuable that an entity owns, benefits from, or has use of, in generating income.

Audit - Quality control: Periodic (usually every six months) onsite-verification (by a certification authority) to ascertain whether or not a documented quality system is being effectively implemented.

Bill of Lading (B/L) – Mostly used for international importation of goods. A document issued by a carrier, or its agent, to the shipper as a contract of carriage of goods. It is also a receipt for cargo accepted for transportation, and must be presented for taking delivery at the destination.

Branding - The process involved in creating a unique name and image for a product in the consumers' mind, mainly through advertising campaigns with a consistent theme. Branding aims to establish a significant and differentiated presence in the market that attracts and retains loyal customers.

Budget - An estimate of costs, revenues, and resources over a specified period, reflecting a reading of future financial conditions and goals. One of the most important administrative tools, a budget serves also as a (1) plan of action for achieving quantified objectives, (2) standard for measuring performance, and (3) device for coping with foreseeable adverse situations.

Capital - Money invested in a business to generate income.

Capitalism - Economic system based (to a varying degree) on private ownership of the factors of production (capital, land, and labor) employed in generation of profits. It is the oldest and most common of all economic systems and, in general, is synonymous with free market system.

Cash flow - Incomings and outgoings of cash, representing the operating activities of an organization.

CEO (b/k/a) Chief Executive Officer - op executive responsible for a firm's overall operations and performance. He or she is the leader of the firm, serves as the main link between the board of directors (the board) and the firm's various parts or levels, and is held solely responsible for the firm's success or failure. One of the major duties of a CEO is to maintain and implement corporate policy, as established by the board. Also called President or managing director, he or she may also be the chairman (or chairperson) of the board.

Certificate of Deposit (CD) - Receipt issued by a depository institution (such as a bank, credit union, or a finance or insurance company) to a depositor who opens a certificate account or time deposit account. Issued in a negotiable or non-negotiable form, it states the (1) amount deposited, (2) rate of interest, and (3) minimum period for which the deposit should be maintained without incurring early withdrawal penalties.

Commerce - Exchange of goods or services for money or in kind, usually on a scale large enough to require transportation from place to place or across city, state, or national boundaries.

Commission - Mutually agreed upon, or fixed by custom or law, fee accruing to an agent, broker, or salesperson for facilitating, initiating, and/ or executing a commercial transaction.

Commodity - A reasonably homogeneous good or material, bought and sold freely as an article of commerce. Commodities include agricultural products, fuels, and metals and are traded in bulk on a commodity exchange or spot market.

Competitor - Any person or entity which is a rival against another. In business, a company in the same industry or a similar industry which offers a similar product or service. The presence of one or more competitors can reduce the prices of goods and services as the companies attempt to gain a larger market share. Competition also requires companies to become more efficient in order to reduce costs.

Contract – A voluntary, deliberate, and legally binding agreement between two or more competent parties. Contracts are usually written but may be spoken or implied, and generally have to do with employment, sale or lease, or tenancy.

Copyright - Legal monopoly that protects published or unpublished original work (for the duration of its author's life plus 50 years) from unauthorized duplication without due credit and compensation.

Corporation - Firm that meets certain legal requirements to be recognized as having a legal existence, as an entity separate and distinct from its owners. Corporations are owned by their stockholders (shareholders) who share in profits and losses generated through the firm's operations, and have three distinct characteristics (1) Legal existence: a firm can (like a person) buy, sell, own, enter into a contract, and sue other persons and firms, and be sued by them. It can do good and be rewarded, and can commit offence and be punished. (2) Limited liability: a firm and its owners are limited in their liability to the creditors and other obligors only up to the resources of the firm, unless the owners give personal-guaranties. (3) Continuity of existence: a firm can live beyond the life spans and capacity of its owners, because its ownership can be transferred through a sale or gift of shares.

Cost – In business, cost is usually a monetary valuation of (1) effort, (2) material, (3) resources, (4) time and utilities consumed, (5) risks incurred, and (6) opportunity forgone in production and delivery of a good or service. All expenses are costs, but not all costs (such as those incurred in acquisition of an income-generating asset) are expenses.

Cross-Branding - A marketing strategy which combines two offerings from separate companies. The technique is usually used to sell complementary products or services. Also called cross promotion or cross merchandising.

Dividend - A share of the after-tax profit of a company, distributed to its shareholders according to the number and class of shares held by them.

Escrow - Arrangement under which a deed, money, security, or other property or document is held by a neutral third-party (called an escrow agent) in trust for a first-party (called grantor, obligor, or promisor) for a specified period or until the occurrence of a condition or event. The escrow agent is duty bound to deliver the asset or document in his or her possession to a named second-party (called grantee, obligee, or promisee) upon the fulfillment of the condition(s) or the happening of a stated event, as established in the escrow agreement.

Ethics - The basic concepts and fundamental principles of decent human conduct. It includes study of universal values such as the essential equality of all men and women, human or natural rights, obedience to the law of land, concern for health and safety and, increasingly, also for the natural environment.

Ex Works – Mostly used when doing business internationally -- Including charges only up to the seller's factory or premises. All charges from there on, such delivery, distribution, and commissions, are to be borne by the buyer.

Exit Strategy - Timing and means with which an investor (usually a venture capitalist) cashes the investment in a startup venture or a buyout arrangement.

Expense - Money spent or cost incurred in an organization's efforts to generate revenue, representing the cost of doing business. Expenses may be in the form of actual cash payments (such as wages and salaries), a computed expired portion (depreciation) of an asset, or an amount taken out of earnings (such as bad debts). Expenses are summarized and charged in the income statement as deductions from the income before assessing income tax. Whereas all expenses are costs, not all costs (such as those incurred in acquisition of income generating assets) are expenses.

Financial Risk - The probability that an actual return on an investment will be lower than the expected return.

Free on Board (FOB) – A term widely used in international trade. Term of sale under which the price invoiced or quoted by a seller includes all charges up to placing the goods on board a ship at the port of departure specified by the buyer. Also called collect freight, freight collect, or freight forward. Definition 2: Used in shipping to indicate that there is no charge to the buyer for goods placed on board a carrier at the point of shipment. Typically followed by the name of a port or city, e.g., F.O.B. San Francisco.

Income - The flow of cash or cash-equivalents received from work (wage or salary), capital (interest or profit), or land (rent). In accounting it means an excess of revenue over expenses for an accounting period. Also called earnings or gross profit.

Inflation - A sustained, rapid increase in prices, as measured by some broad index (such as Consumer Price Index) over months or years, and mirrored in the correspondingly decreasing purchasing power of the currency. It has its worst effect on the fixed-wage earners, and is a disincentive to save.

Intellectual Property - Knowledge, creative ideas, or expressions of human mind that have commercial value and are protectable under copyright, patent, servicemark, trademark, or trade secret laws from imitation, infringement, and dilution. Intellectual property includes brand names, discoveries, formulas, inventions, knowledge, registered designs, software, and works of artistic, literary, or musical nature. It is one of the most readily tradable properties in the digital marketplace.

Interest - A fee paid for the use of another party's money. To the borrower it is the cost of renting money, to the lender the income from lending it.

Inventory - An itemized catalog or list of tangible goods or property, or the intangible attributes or qualities.

Key Person Insurance - Life and/or disability insurance on one (or more) key persons whose loss or unavailability may cause loss of profit, goodwill, or increase in expenses. These insurance policies help finance the search and training of a successor, or compensate for fall in profits.

Letter of Credit (L/C) - A written commitment to pay, by a buyer's or importer's bank (called the issuing bank) to the seller's or exporter's bank (called the accepting bank, negotiating bank, or paying bank). A letter of credit guarantees payment of a specified sum in a specified currency, provided the seller meets precisely-defined conditions and submits the prescribed documents within a fixed timeframe. These documents almost always include a clean bill of lading or air waybill, commercial invoice, and certificate of origin.

Leverage - The ability to influence a system, or an environment, in a way that multiplies the outcome of one's efforts without a corresponding increase in the consumption of resources. In other words, leverage is the advantageous condition of having a relatively small amount of cost yield a relatively high level of returns.

Liability - Accounts and wages payable, accrued rent and taxes, trade debt, and short and long-term loans. Owners' equity is also termed a liability because it is an obligation of the company to its owners.

Marketing Strategy - An organization's strategy that combines all of its marketing goals into one comprehensive plan. A good marketing strategy should be drawn from market research and focus on the right product mix in order to achieve the maximum profit potential and sustain the business. The marketing strategy is the foundation of a marketing plan.

Operations - Jobs or tasks consisting of one or more elements or subtasks, performed typically in one location.

Ownership - The ultimate and exclusive right conferred by a lawful claim or title, and subject to certain restrictions to enjoy, occupy, possess, rent, sell, use, give away, or even destroy an item of property.

Payment terms - The conditions under which a seller will complete a sale.

Typically, these terms specify the period allowed to a buyer to pay off the amount due, and may demand cash in advance, cash on delivery, a deferred payment period of 30 days or more, or other similar provisions.

Pro forma Invoice - An abridged or estimated invoice sent by a seller to a buyer in advance of a shipment or delivery of goods. It notes the kind and quantity of goods, their value, and other important information such as weight and transportation charges. Pro forma invoices are commonly used as preliminary invoices with a quotation, or for customs purposes in importation. They differ from a normal invoice in not being a demand or request for payment.

Purchase Order (PO) - A buyer-generated document that authorizes a purchase transaction. When accepted by the seller, it becomes a contract binding on both parties. A purchase order sets forth the descriptions, quantities, prices, discounts, payment terms, date of performance or shipment, other associated terms and conditions, and identifies a specific seller.

Revenue - The income generated from sale of goods or services, or any other use of capital or assets, associated with the main operations of an organization before any costs or expenses are deducted. Revenue is shown usually as the top item in an income (profit and loss) statement from which all charges, costs, and expenses are subtracted to arrive at net income.

Serial Entrepreneur - An entrepreneur who continuously comes up with new ideas and starts new businesses. As opposed to a typical entrepreneur, who will often come up with an idea, start the company, and then see it through and play an important role in the day to day functioning of the new company, a serial entrepreneur will often come up with the idea and get things started, but then give responsibility to someone else and move on to a new idea and a new venture. This can be a good thing if the individual has lots of unique ideas and is the best one suited to get each one started, but can be a bad thing if the individual stops putting time into a company that needs his or her help, in order to try to move forward with a new idea that may or may not succeed.

Social Entrepreneur - Independent business individuals that act as agents of change for the society. They will work to improve innovative approaches to existing systems by seizing opportunities others have missed. They work to develop sustainable solutions for the purpose of changing society for the better.

Sweat Equity - Increased worth of a business (over and above the money invested) created by the unpaid mental and/or physical hard work of the founder/owner.

Valuation – Appraising or estimating the worth of the business.

CHRONICLES OF A BO$$!

Your blueprint to creating a life of independence, freedom and wealth!

RESOURCES

A list of websites that will help you on your quest to creating a life of independence, freedom, and wealth.

www.7cupsoftea.com –7 Cups of Tea is an on-demand emotional health and well-being service geared towards Entrepreneurs.

www.99designs.com - #1 Marketplace for graphic design, including logo design, web design and other design contests.

www.AbetterLemonadeStand.com - A Better Lemonade Stand in an online ecommerce incubator. Its purpose is to inspire new entrepreneurs as well as to provide the tools and resources to build, launch and grow online businesses better, faster and cheaper.

www.BlogTrepreneur.com - Blogtrepreneur.com is a leading Entrepreneurship Blog, helping you turn your entrepreneurial dream into a reality with the absolute latest tips, news and advice!

www.BudgetsAreSexy.com - A money blog trying to spice things up a bit! We rock out budget planning, retirement, credit cards, 401k, templates & becoming a millionaire.

www.ChroniclesOfABoss.com – Toyiah Marquis' quest to living life outside the box!

www.Copyright.gov - U.S. Copyright Office is an office of public record for copyright registration and deposit of copyright material.

www.Entrepreneur.com - Advice, insight, profiles and guides for established and aspiring entrepreneurs worldwide.

www.Eofire.com - EntrepreneurOnFire is an award winning Podcast where John Lee Dumas chats with today's most inspiring Entrepreneurs 7-days a week.

www.Etsy.com - Buy and sell handmade or vintage items, art and supplies on Etsy, the world's most vibrant handmade marketplace.

www.Fiverr.com - Graphics, marketing, fun, and more online services, on budget and on time.

www.GoDaddy.com – World's Largest Domain Registrar.

www.HelpAReporter.com - Help a Reporter connects news sources with journalists looking for their expertise.

www.Hootsuite.com - Enhance your social media management with Hootsuite, the leading social media dashboard.

www.iBrandMatchmaker.com - International Importing, Brand Development, and Consulting Services

www.irs.gov/Businesses/Small-Businesses-&-Self-Employed/Starting-a-Business - Get your business an EIN # and other helpful steps and resources you need by visiting the IRS's small business center online.

www.Kickstarter.com - Kickstarter is the world's largest funding platform for creative projects. A home for film, music, art, theater, games, comics, design, photography, and more.

www.MyWifeQuitHerJob.com - When my wife became pregnant with our first child, she decided to quit her job. We started an online store and made over $100K in 12 months to replace her salary. Learn how you can do the same thing we did.

www.SBA.gov – Small business administration: An electronic gateway of procurement information for and about small businesses.

www.SeanOgle.com - Hey, this is Sean Ogle, creator and founder of Location 180. I've spent the last five years of my life learning how to travel and work from anywhere in the world.

www.Shopify.com – Ecommerce solution for opening your own online store.

www.SmartPassiveIncome.com - Learn how to build an online passive income business with Pat Flynn.

www.SparkandHustle.com - Spark & Hustle, a community of women entrepreneurs and small business owners, turning passion to profit.

www.TheElevatorLife.com - We are entrepreneurs running businesses and living in southern China. The goal of of T.E.L. is to pass along our experiences to help others do the same thing!

www.ThePennyHoarder.com – Winning ways to get paid!

www.TierraDestinyReid.com - TDR Brands International helps women unlock their maximum potential in business by adopting conscious living and intentional leadership best practices.

www.Upwork.com - Find freelancers and freelance jobs on Upwork - the world's largest online workplace where savvy businesses and professional freelancers go to work!

www.USPTO.gov - United States Patent and Trademark Office's main web site.

www.Weebly.com - Weebly makes it surprisingly easy to create a high-quality website, blog or online store.

www.Wordpress.com - Create a free website or easily build a blog.

www.ingramcontent.com/pod-product-compliance
Lightning Source LLC
Chambersburg PA
CBHW022047210326
41519CB00055B/854